Working with
Behavioral Disorders

Social Skills for Students with Autism

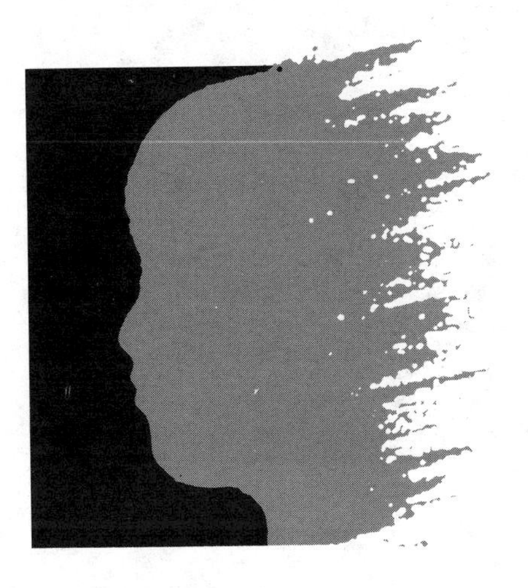

Richard L. Simpson,
Brenda Smith Myles, Gary M. Sasso,
and Debra M. Kamps

Published by The Council for Exceptional Children

Library of Congress Cataloging-in-Publication Data

Social skills for students with autism / Richard L. Simpson ... [et al.].
p. cm.
"CEC mini-library."
Includes bibliographical references.
ISBN 0-86586-202-8 (pbk.)
1. Autistic children—Education—United States. 2. Social skills—Study and teaching—United States. 3. Peer-group tutoring of students—United States. I. Simpson, Richard L., 1945- .
LC4718.S66 1991
371.94—dc20 91-9006
CIP

ISBN 0-86586-202-8

Stock No. P343

Printed in the United States of America
10 9 8 7 6 5 4 3 2 1

Contents

Foreword

Working with Behavioral Disorders CEC Mini-Library

One of the greatest underserved populations in the schools today is students who have severe emotional and behavioral problems. These students present classroom teachers and other school personnel with the challenges of involving them effectively in the learning process and facilitating their social and emotional development.

The editors have coordinated a series of publications that address a number of critical issues facing service providers in planning and implementing more appropriate programs for children and youth with severe emotional and behavioral problems. There are nine booklets in this Mini-Library series, each one designed for a specific purpose.

- *Teaching Students with Behavioral Disorders: Basic Questions and Answers* addresses questions that classroom teachers commonly ask about instructional issues, classroom management, teacher collaboration, and assessment and identification of students with emotional and behavioral disorders.
- *Conduct Disorders and Social Maladjustments: Policies, Politics, and Programming* examines the issues associated with providing services to students who exhibit externalizing or acting-out behaviors in the schools.
- *Behaviorally Disordered? Assessment for Identification and Instruction* discusses systematic screening procedures and the need for functional assessment procedures that will facilitate provision of services to students with emotional and behavioral disorders.

- *Preparing to Integrate Students with Behavioral Disorders* provides guidelines to assist in the integration of students into mainstream settings and the delivery of appropriate instructional services to these students.
- *Teaching Young Children with Behavioral Disorders* highlights the applications of Public Law 99–457 for young children with special needs and delineates a variety of interventions that focus on both young children and their families.
- *Reducing Undesirable Behaviors* provides procedures to reduce undesirable behavior in the schools and lists specific recommendations for using these procedures.
- *Social Skills for Students with Autism* presents information on using a variety of effective strategies for teaching social skills to children and youth with autism.
- *Special Education in Juvenile Corrections* highlights the fact that a large percentage of youth incarcerated in juvenile correctional facilities has special learning, social, and emotional needs. Numerous practical suggestions are delineated for providing meaningful special education services in these settings.
- *Moving On: Transitions for Youth with Behavioral Disorders* presents practical approaches to working with students in vocational settings and provides examples of successful programs and activities.

We believe that this Mini-Library series will be of great benefit to those endeavoring to develop new programs or enhance existing programs for students with emotional and behavioral disorders.

Lyndal M. Bullock
Robert B. Rutherford, Jr.

Introduction

Knowledge and information about autism have increased significantly since the time of Kanner's (1943) seminal writing; however, many of his observations about the syndrome remain relevant. In particular, experts agree that children and youth with autism are characterized by difficulty in developing and maintaining appropriate interpersonal relationships and by a lack of interest in and responsiveness to others (Koegel, Rincover, & Egel, 1982; Rumsey, Rapoport, & Sceery, 1985; Rutter & Schopler, 1987; Shores, 1987).

Children and youth with autism also frequently have developmental delays, obsessive desire for sameness, aberrant speech and language development, and atypical reactions to environmental events, including manifestation of stereotypic and other nonfunctional repetitive actions and responses. Social deficits, however, are often considered to be the most significant disability with which children and youth with autism must contend (Gaylord-Ross, Haring, Breen, & Pitts-Conway, 1984; Sasso, Simpson, & Novak, 1985). In fact, Kanner (1943) originally used the term *autistic* to describe children's inability to relate and their strong preference for being left alone.

Evidence for the relative significance of social deficits in children with autism is in part based on parental reports. Parents of autistic infants and young children often observe that their offspring are indifferent to attention and are generally oblivious to others; they even question their children's ability to hear. Individuals with autism often avoid eye contact and isolate themselves socially. They typically form few close friendships outside their immediate family, and even higher-functioning individuals with autism tend to be perceived as socially peculiar (Tsai & Scott-Miller, 1988).

In a follow-up of the 11 children diagnosed as having autism in the original study, Kanner (1971) reported that as adults these persons failed to outgrow their social isolation and awkwardness. Others (Gilliam, 1981; Rutter & Schopler, 1987; Simpson & Regan, 1986) have also noted that children and youth with autism have myriad social problems and deficits. Accordingly, goals for these individuals are often similar to those suggested by Neel (1986): "To increase the ability of autistic children to control and participate in their environment" (p. 1). The need for social skills development of autistic children is also based on findings that the ability to make appropriate and functional social initiations and responses correlates positively with long-term success in living and working in normalized environments (Lovaas, 1987; McEvoy & Odom, 1987; Shapiro, Chiarandini, & Fish, 1974; Wehman & Kregel, 1988).

Recognition of the importance of improving the quantity and quality of social interactions of autistic children and youth has existed for some time. Thus, it is not surprising that methods and procedures to facilitate social interactions between individuals with autism and others are increasingly being made a part of students' programs. In this context, *social interaction* refers to establishing and maintaining positive social relations with others, including making appropriate social initiations and appropriately responding to social initiations of others.

Historical and Empirical Considerations

A variety of philosophical and theoretical changes have occurred in the 20 years during which social interactions of children and youth with autism have been studied. Moreover, strategies, expectations, and goals that facilitate appropriate responses of students with autism have undergone significant modification. Social interactions originally were touted to be monadic in nature. That is, early researchers generally focused on children's discrete social responses, with only limited reference to the impact these acts had on others. Thus, Shores (1987) noted that early social interaction studies measured " . . . discreet responses . . . without direct reference to the functional effects of those responses on the peers' behavior" (p. 234). Later studies employed a dyadic view, acknowledging that social interactions were reciprocal—with one person reinforcing another at equitable rates (Shores, 1987; Strain & Timm, 1974).

Early social interaction instruction of children and youth with autism focused almost exclusively on using an operant learning approach to modify and remediate behavioral excesses and deficits (Egel, Richman, & Koegel, 1981; Strain, Cooke, & Apolloni, 1976; Strain, Shores, & Timm, 1977). Emphasis was placed on increasing the quantity of appropriate behavior and decreasing the quantity of behavioral excesses (Simpson, 1987; Strain, Shores, & Kerr, 1976); measures of quality (e.g., choice-making, social appropriateness, social interest) were given little consideration (Guess & Siegel-Causey, 1985; Schopler & Mesibov, 1983).

Current efforts in this area are focused on improving both the quality and quantity of students' social interactions (Peck, 1985).

Increased attention also has been given to the environment in which social interactions occur (Peck, 1985). University and laboratory facilities were used primarily in early studies, offering structured, segregated, and somewhat artificial settings for teaching, demonstrating, and generalizing social responses (Gaylord-Ross & Haring, 1987). More recent efforts have involved social interaction instruction in naturalistic settings, including home, community, and schools in which students with disabilities and those without are integrated (Lord & Hopkins, 1986; Simpson, 1987). The use of integrated, naturalistic settings was born, at least in part, out of the recognition that it was necessary to structure skill generalization. Indeed, one of the consistent findings in the early social interaction literature was the absence of generalized behavior. Thus, transient, setting-specific treatment effects were reported in many early social interaction instructional programs (Stokes & Baer, 1977). Although some researchers continue to suggest that the importance of teaching generalization is poorly recognized (Strain, 1983), there is no doubt that generalization is of major concern in most current social interaction instructional programs (McConnell, 1987; Simpson, 1987).

Researchers debate whether adult-mediated or peer-mediated interventions more effectively improve the social behavior of students with autism (Sasso, 1987). Adult-mediated procedures—those that rely on an adult to evoke or prompt appropriate social behavior—were used almost exclusively in early social interaction instructional programs, and they remain prominent today (Guess & Siegel-Causey, 1985). Some critics contend that adult mediation disrupts social activities, makes students prompt dependent, and interferes with social spontaneity (Odom & Strain, 1986; Strain & Fox, 1981); nonetheless, such programs clearly have been shown to promote social interaction (Shores, 1987). Mirenda (cited in Peck, 1985) reported that a high level of teacher mediation resulted in increased rates of student-initiated interactions and question-asking in 12 adolescents with autism. Similar results have been reported by others (i.e., Meyer et al., 1987; Peck, 1985; Odom & Strain, 1986; Strain & Timm, 1974; Strain, Cooke, & Appolloni, 1976).

A number of researchers and practitioners posit that peer-mediated social interaction programs (i.e., those that involve teaching children to initiate and prompt social behaviors, including sharing, playing, assisting, and conversing) offer a number of advantages. Such techniques, according to Strain, Odom, and McConnell (1984), do not disrupt natural social exchanges and are minimally intrusive. Ragland, Kerr, and Strain (1978) reported increases in children's positive social interactions, including skill generalization among nontargeted children, using a peer-mediated procedure. Moreover, investigators have found that peer-initiated interventions are effective in increasing social responses of children with autism (Lord & Hopkins, 1986; Odom, Hoyson, Jamieson, & Strain, 1985; Odom, Strain, Karger, & Smith, 1986; Sasso et al., 1985).

Debate over social interaction instruction also involves discussion of whether programming should be primarily structured around instructional or noninstructional activities. Instruction-based programs include peer-tutoring, wherein students with mild or no disabilities serve as tutors for children and youth with autism and other disabilities (Gaylord-Ross & Haring, 1987; Gaylord-Ross & Pitts-Conway, 1984). Such programs have resulted in skill development as well as opportunities for normally achieving students and students with disabilities to interact. These programs also have been shown to improve attitudes of normally achieving students toward their peers with disabilities (Fiedler & Simpson, 1987).

Other professionals advocate for noninstructional social interaction programs, basing their preference on the alleged advantages of structuring interactions around social or recreational activities rather than academic or skill development programs (Sasso, 1987; Shores, 1987; Strain, 1982). Advocates of noninstructional programming contend that these programs provide opportunities for students with autism to practice appropriate social interaction behaviors in an environment in which the skills are likely to be used. Additionally, advocates indicate that involving normally achieving students in leisure, recreational, or overtly social activities promotes appropriate social development and positive attitude formation toward individuals with disabilities.

Debate over the advantages of instructional and noninstructional social interaction formats most likely will continue. However, it should be noted that both efforts have been shown to have a positive influence on the social behavior of students with autism. Thus, it is our opinion that both types of programs can be used to promote appropriate social contact between students with autism and others.

The primary purpose of this publication is to identify and discuss methods and procedures to facilitate appropriate social interactions between children and youth with autism and others. It is designed for practitioners, specifically to provide information and techniques useful in designing social interaction programs.

1. Promoting Social Development

Four approaches commonly have been used to promote social development in children and youth with autism: direct skill instruction, antecedent prompting procedures, peer-initiation strategies, and peer tutoring.

For individuals with autism, the development of reciprocal social interactions and relationships can be conceptualized as an interrelationship among a number of relevant variables. These include the number, type, setting, and distribution of peer social interactions. That is, the techniques used to increase social competence should (a) yield interactions at a rate similar to that found in the child's environments, (b) include cooperative components, and (c) take advantage of age-appropriate activities. Efforts also should be made to generalize social interactions across settings and persons. Specifically, these social behaviors should be related to the array of settings and social opportunities available to individuals with autism, which include *friendships, work, leisure, family, school,* and other *casual* social contacts.

Since the ultimate goal of social interaction programs is to increase contact between students with disabilities and those without, receptive attitudes are essential. Information and discussions allow for the formation of more positive attitudes toward students with autism. In this regard, materials such as the *Autism Fact Sheet* (NIH Publication #88-1877), obtainable through most local chapters of the Autism Society of America, and Simpson and Regan's (1986) curriculum on children with autism (designed for socially competent students) are helpful in describing student characteristics and fostering positive attitude development. Other resources such as slide presentations on autism, videotapes of students with autism, and individual profiles can also help set the stage for effective social interaction programs.

An additional factor that should be considered is the social validity of the interactions that are fostered by various interventions (Kazdin, 1977). Within this context, social validity refers to procedures whose outcomes are viewed as important *and* beneficial to the individual with autism, nondisabled peers, parents, school, and community. The central concern is the social importance of the behavior change to the consumers. In others words, do social interaction variables facilitate increases in friendships or relationships between individuals with autism and the important people in their environment?

The literature of the last 10 years suggests four distinct paths to promoting the social development of school-aged children and youth with autism. One of the most intrusive procedures is *direct instruction* of relevant social behaviors that relies on the overt manipulation of task-analyzed skills to promote higher frequencies of social behavior (Gaylord-Ross & Haring, 1987). A second type of intervention that has been used involves *antecedent prompting* or teacher mediation of social interactions (McEvoy & Odom, 1987). The most typical form of this technique is the delivery of an initiation prompt by the teacher followed by reinforcement (attention or praise) to the child with autism for successful engagement in positive social interaction with a peer (Fox, Shores, Linderman, & Strain, 1986; Odom & Strain, 1986). A third procedure is known as *peer initiation.* This process involves teaching socially competent peers to initiate interactions with individuals with autism (Ragland, Kerr, & Strain, 1978; Sasso & Rude, 1987). A fourth method for increasing social interactions between students with autism and their socially competent peers is *peer tutoring*. This program not only structures interactions between socially competent students and those with autism but also provides additional skill development opportunities for children and youth with autism (Gaylord-Ross & Haring, 1987).

2. Direct Skill Instruction

This approach first identifies social skills that need to be developed, then determines the steps required to build those skills and provides practice in a variety of settings.

Most of the social skills programs for autistic individuals have incorporated three major components: initial task analyses of skills considered important to the child in natural settings; sequential teaching of each of the task-analyzed steps to criterion using modeling, repeated trials, prompts, and reinforcement with peers in the natural environment; and a multiple-exemplars approach to cross-setting generalization (Sasso, Melloy, & Kavale, 1990; Stokes & Baer, 1977). For example, Gaylord-Ross and others (1984) taught autistic adolescents to effectively use age-appropriate games (i.e., radios, videogames) and leisure materials (i.e., chewing gum) through task analyses and verbal-physical prompts. Independent completion of the entire task analysis resulted in reinforcement. Following this initial object instruction, the autistic adolescents were taught to initiate interactions with peers to engage in the activities they had learned. This instruction involved the use of socially competent peers, an instructional script that made use of role play, and eventual introduction of peers with autism. Several peers were used to successfully transfer the skills across persons. A similar procedure was used by Breen, Haring, Pitts-Conway, and Gaylord-Ross (1985) to teach appropriate social interactions within the context of work environments.

There are several advantages to direct social instruction procedures. First, the individual with autism gains significantly in independence, with more control over the time and place of social interactions. Second, the games become associated with social initiations and responses when paired with concurrent instruction in social interactions and repeated practice. That is, the games begin to act as prompts for social interaction. Finally and most important, instruction that uses task and prompt/reinforcement strategies repeatedly has been shown to be an effective social interaction intervention for even the most socially withdrawn children and youth with autism.

There is, however, one primary disadvantage to the use of a direct instruction approach to social competence. Research suggests that each stable social environment (e.g., classroom, workplace) represents an individualized set of local norms for socially appropriate and facilitative behavior (Bem & Lord, 1979). For example, Sasso, Hughes, Swanson, and Novak (1987) found that the initial instruction of confederates to reinforce other socially competent peers following positive interactions with a student with autism resulted in behavior that was not reinforcing to the peers. By directly teaching skills outside the context of these norms, we may significantly reduce the probability that the skills will be naturally reinforced and thus "trapped" (Kohler & Greenwood, 1986; McConnell, 1987) by preferred social environments. Therefore, use of social skills direct instruction in combination with other social interaction instruction is desirable.

3. Antecedent Prompting Procedures

In this approach the teacher prompts the child to engage in some kind of interactive behavior, which, if it occurs, is responded to positively by classmates and the teacher.

This procedure, also known as *teacher mediation,* involves two distinct processes (Odom & Strain, 1986). First, the student with autism is paired with a socially competent peer in a play setting. The peer usually is instructed to remain in proximity to the student with autism and play *if* the student initiates or otherwise signals a desire to engage in social interaction. Second, the teacher remains in the play area and provides periodic verbal prompts to the child with autism to engage in one of a variety of interaction behaviors (e.g., sharing, offering to engage in an activity). The teacher then waits a reasonable period of time (e.g., 5 seconds) for a response. If the student responds, the teacher provides praise and encouragement. If the child fails to respond, the teacher generally repeats the verbal prompt and physically assists the child to engage in the social initiation.

In the last few years, investigators have established that antecedent prompting procedures can be effective for children with autism (Odom & Strain, 1986). An increasingly used modification of the basic antecedent procedure involves the use of teacher-mediated group affection activities to promote positive social interaction (McEvoy & Odom, 1987). In this program, children with autism and socially competent children are involved in typical preschool games, songs, and materials. Initially, the children are prompted to greet each other by exchanging some form of physical affection such as a hug or pat on the back. The children then participate in the games or activities that are modified to include an affection component. For example, a group song such as "If You're Happy and You Know It Clap Your Hands" might be changed to "If You're Happy and You Know It Tickle Your Friend." The benefits of this modified antecedent prompting procedure include a greater frequency of social interaction during the affection activities that appears to generalize and maintain in nontreatment settings (Twardosz, Nordquist, Simon, & Botkin, 1983), desensitization to peer interaction, and exposure to natural social interactions with competent peers in freeplay situations.

Over all, these teacher-mediated procedures have been found to increase levels of social interaction, often above those found with peer-initiation strategies. These techniques are most effective when they include repeated exposure to competent peers in normalized environments. Finally, there is some emerging evidence that modifications of these procedures may result in generalization to other settings (Fox, Gunter, Brady, Bambara, Spiegel-McGill, & Shores, 1984).

There are also drawbacks to the use of these techniques (Sasso, 1987). Strain and Fox (1981) reported that teacher prompts can disrupt ongoing social exchanges, resulting in brief, sometimes stilted interactions. In addition, Odom and Strain (1986) compared antecedent prompting to peer initiation strategies and found that the children with autism became prompt dependent, initiating and responding only when instructed to do so by the teacher. Finally, Voeltz (1982) suggested that, when prompted to initiate and instruct, peers may perceive themselves as teachers rather than as friends. This drawback was at least in part supported by Sasso, Mitchell, and Struthers (1986), who compared academic tutoring to social interaction activities for students with autism. These researchers found that although tutoring resulted in high levels of interaction, the interactions tended to be instructional rather than social.

4. Peer-Initiated Strategies

With these strategies socially competent peers are taught how to initiate and encourage social interactions with children with autism in natural settings.

Peer-mediated social interaction procedures have been used for a number of years, initially with withdrawn preschool children (Strain, Shores, & Timm, 1977), but also with more severely involved children with autism and mental disabilities (Ragland, Kerr, & Strain, 1978; Sasso & Rude, 1987). Socially competent peers are taught to initiate social interactions with children with autism. They are subsequently paired in natural settings for social activities. The most direct outcome of these procedures has been an increase in positive social responses by children with autism. This outcome is important because of the strong, positive association between social responses and peer acceptance (Sasso, 1987).

A number of modifications to peer-initiated techniques appear to increase the effectiveness of these procedures for individuals with autism. Sasso and Rude (1987) found that teaching high-status peers to interact with students with autism increased the number of positive social interactions. Moreover, untrained peers in the same setting also increased their social interactions with the students with autism. The result was modest yet consistent increases in the response rate, initiation, and length of interactions of participants with autism.

Another modification of peer-initiated interventions involves the use of triads composed of two peers and one child with autism. The rationale for such an arrangement is that there is typically a level of "dead time" within a dyadic pairing due to the often limited communication skills of children with autism. Triads have been viewed as a way to overcome this weakness and provide higher levels of social initiations to individuals with autism. An initial comparison of peer dyads and triads revealed that, although there were higher levels of social interactions within the triad, many of the interactions excluded the child with autism. However, interactions still occurred between socially competent participants and those with autism. It remains unclear what imitative effects may occur for the child with autism as a result of close proximity to the social interactions of competent peers. Additional work is needed to clarify the effects of peer triad techniques (Sasso, 1989).

There are several advantages to the use of peer-initiated interventions. First, they demand the use of natural social interaction environments and contexts. Second, valid interaction behaviors are ensured because these programs depend on the typical social interaction behaviors of socially competent peers. These techniques are also easy and time efficient in terms of instruction and administration. Finally, and most important, peer-initiated interventions have resulted in increased levels of initiations and responses from both participants with autism and competent peers as well as evidence of longer lasting interactions (Sasso, 1987).

The major weakness of peer-initiation programs is that there is currently little evidence of generalization and maintenance of interactions (McEvoy & Odom, 1987). In addition, prompts are sometimes necessary to ensure that the competent peer remains in contact with the child with autism, which can result in the problems associated with antecedent prompting interventions.

5. Peer Tutoring

This approach has socially competent peers learn how to use effective teaching techniques and positive reinforcement to teach academic subjects to classmates with autism.

Peer tutoring programs represent a viable means of improving the curricular and social interaction skills of students with autism. Research reveals that the teaching of specific tutoring strategies facilitates interaction among children with autism and their socially competent peers. These studies indicate that effects of social initiation intervention are immediately evident and substantial (Blew, Schwartz, & Luce, 1985; Egel et al., 1981; Goldstein & Strain, 1988; Strain, 1983).

In peer tutoring sessions, students work in dyads with socially competent peers typically serving as tutors and students with autism taking the role of tutee. Tutoring sessions are structured, with both tutor and tutee having assigned roles.

The first step in establishing a peer tutoring program is scheduling informal interaction periods between students with autism and their socially competent peers. It is important that students have some interaction experiences and familiarity with each other. Additionally, peers must be aware of the basic characteristics of the students with autism. Group and individual instruction of tutors can then begin.

Group instruction involves teachers' explanations of procedures for working with students on various learning tasks. In particular, teachers describe (a) what tasks and materials to use in tutoring, (b) how to give directions, (c) how to give reinforcement, and (d) how to manage inappropriate behavior. Accordingly, tutors are taught to give short, clearly stated directions (e.g., "Point to the shoe," "Read this word") and to model correct responses (e.g., labeling objects, using noun-verb phrases).

The importance of reinforcement as a major component of successful tutoring is emphasized. Tutors are taught to reinforce appropriate behavior by using frequent positive statements (e.g., "Good counting," "That's right, it's a ball"). To manage behaviors during sessions, tutors also are taught to use verbal prompts (e.g., stating, "Look at your book" when the tutee is not attending), physical guidance (e.g., touching the tutee's arm to encourage beginning a task), and ignoring (e.g., attending to a separate task when the tutee displays inappropriate behavior).

Tutors also are informed that their role involves both privilege and responsibility. Thus, each tutor is provided the following role-related information:

1. Tutors have sole responsibility for teaching a given task to another student.
2. Tutors must attend every scheduled tutoring session on days they are in school.
3. Students with autism depend on tutors in two ways: to teach them and to befriend them.
4. Students with autism imitate, so tutors need to be good role models and behave in an appropriate manner.
5. Tutors and tutees are taught to work first, then play. That is, pairs engage in assigned tasks for approximately 20 minutes, then play for approximately 10 minutes.

Subsequent to general tutoring sessions the teacher provides individual tutor instruction in the following areas: (a) the academic subject area for tutoring; (b) materials and activities for tutoring; (c) demonstrations in tutoring by the teacher working with students with autism; (d) a practice session on tutoring with students under teacher supervision; (e) teacher feedback on the tutor's performance; and (f) data collection. Students must demonstrate tutoring competencies prior to tutoring peers with autism.

Tutoring Sessions

Tutoring sessions should be scheduled a minimum of 3 days per week for approximately 30-minute time periods. Sessions should be structured to include both instruction and free play. Freeplay sessions generally occur following instruction; thus, providing the tutee an opportunity to practice social interaction skills.

A typical tutoring session involves the following components:

1. The tutors arrive and greet tutees.

2. The tutors to go the materials area and gather test items.
3. The tutors and tutees sit at the tutees' desks and begin academic tutoring.
4. The teacher moves among pairs, providing feedback or assistance as needed.
5. The tutors collect data on tutees' performance (approximately 5 minutes per student, at least once per week).
6. At the end of approximately 20 minutes, the teacher announces time for free play.
7. The tutors return the academic materials and choose a play activity.
8. The tutors engage in social activity at the tutees' desks or a designated play area.
9. At the end of approximately 10 minutes of free play, the teacher announces that it is time for tutors to return to their classes.
10. Peer tutors and students with autism say goodbye.

The teacher's role during tutoring and freeplay sessions is to monitor each pair, provide feedback to tutors, reinforce desired behaviors, and collect tutoring data. Periodically, the teacher will need to review procedures, organize new academic tasks, or deal with specific behavior issues.

Peer tutoring programs are becoming increasingly commonplace. Both regular and special educators are recognizing these programs as a means for fostering integration and increasing learning activities. Tutors can be used to facilitate academic growth and development in a variety of areas, including oral reading, word recognition, comprehension, coin recognition and value, and receptive/expressive language skills (Gaylord-Ross & Pitts-Conway, 1984; Kamps, Locke, Delquadri, & Hall, 1989). Peer tutoring is an efficient means of increasing interactions between individuals with disabilities and those without. For example, Blew and others (1985) found that a peer tutoring program successfully increased the interactions of children with autism with others in their environment.

A potential weakness of peer tutoring is that it creates inequitable relationships between students with disabilities and their nondisabled peers. That is, rather than creating an environment for mutually beneficial interactions, peer tutoring sets up a relationship in which one student is in control of another.

6. Considerations for Social Interaction Programming

- ***Match social interaction programs to students' needs and settings.***
- ***Establish reasonable social interaction expectations.***
- ***Be sensitive to local social interaction norms and conditions.***
- ***Program for interaction quality as well as quantity.***
- ***Recognize that not all regular class students will be appropriate for social interaction programs.***
- ***Reduce aberrant behaviors prior to initiating social interaction programs.***
- ***Provide ongoing instruction and monitoring.***
- ***Task analyze social interaction skills.***
- ***Consider the importance of setting and material variables.***
- ***Consider social validity in programming.***
- ***Prioritize social interaction skills.***
- ***Tailor reinforcement to meet individual needs.***
- ***Educate tutors and others about autism.***
- ***Facilitate initial interactions.***
- ***Make data-based program decisions.***
- ***Generalize social skills.***
- ***Maintain acquired social skills.***

A. Match Social Interaction Programs to Students' Needs and Settings

Just like socially competent students, children and youth with autism differ in a number of ways. Similarly, schools and classrooms have unique characteristics, attitudes, and norms. Programs for facilitating social interactions between socially competent students and pupils with autism must accordingly vary with circumstances, situations, and needs. Thus, educators must consider many options to stimulate interactions between these groups. For instance, peer tutoring may be more appropriate in some settings and with certain students than others. Similarly, some students will be more responsive to antecedent prompting than others. Selection of social interaction procedures based on individual subject, setting, and other salient variables increases the likelihood of successful outcomes.

B. Establish Reasonable Social Interaction Expectations

Social interaction programs are designed to enhance relationships between children and youth with autism and their socially competent classmates. Increased social interaction enhances acceptance of individuals with disabilities, facilitates the social skill development of students with disabilities, and promotes positive community attitudes toward disabilities. It is unrealistic, however, to think that social interaction programs will lead to intimate friendships between regular class students and their peers with autism. Such relationships are based on mutual interests, compatibility, and other factors rarely present in associations between students with autism and their socially competent peers. This is not intended to take away from the significance of interactions between students with and without disabilities, the importance of regular class students' being accepting and responsive to their peers with autism, or the necessity for children and youth with autism to make appropriate initiations and responses to others. Rather, it is intended to be a reminder that social interaction goals must be commensurate with the relationships that may ensue.

C. Be Sensitive to Local Social Interaction Norms and Conditions

Educators must establish social interaction programs, contingencies, expectations, and procedures that coincide with the characteristics of individual settings. That is, instructional methods are most effective when they allow students to interact in regularly occurring activities in accordance with established local norms. For instance, teaching a student with autism to talk to her socially competent peers during activities when students ordinarily do not talk may be counterproductive to the goal of encouraging social interactions.

D. Program for Interaction Quality as Well as Quantity

Researchers have documented clearly the necessity of attending to the quality of social initiations and responses as well as quantity (Shores, 1987). Teachers and others who organize social interaction programs must recognize that the frequency or duration with which a child with autism interacts with socially competent peers may not be nearly as important as the level at which the interaction occurs. That is, a rehearsed, stilted conversational response of 15 words may not be as meaningful as a 5-word spontaneously generated statement. Accordingly, instructional methods and evaluation techniques must focus on both qualitative and quantitative aspects of social interactions.

E. Recognize That Not All Regular Class Students Will Be Appropriate for Social Interaction Programs

Unfortunate as it may be, not all children and adolescents are appropriate for social interaction programs. Regular class students who express reluctance or a dislike for involvement with students with autism and students who have demonstrated poor role model qualities or who otherwise have interacted poorly with students with autism may be excluded. This is not to suggest that regular class students who have learning and behavior problems automatically should be excluded from social interaction program consideration. A number of such students have shown themselves to be excellent peer confederates and tutors, in spite of their own problems. Nonetheless, educators must closely evaluate each student for social interaction program participation and select only those individuals who are suitable for interacting with children and youth with autism.

F. Reduce Aberrant Behaviors Prior to Initiating Social Interaction Programs

It is unrealistic to assume that regular class children and youth will interact with students who routinely hit them, scream at them, or otherwise emit highly deviant behavior. Accordingly, educators and other professionals must bring the behavior of pupils with autism under control prior to initiating social interaction programs with regular class students. Individuals with autism need not be free of all self-stimulatory and other negative behaviors; however, basic compliance must be established prior to initiating social interaction programs.

G. Provide Ongoing Instruction and Monitoring

Regular class students and pupils with autism interact most effectively when provided continual instruction and feedback. That is, social interaction instruction must not be viewed as a process wherein initial instruction and supervision are sufficient to achieve social interaction goals and objectives. Rather, teachers and other professionals must provide ongoing instruction and supervision.

H. Task Analyze Social Interaction Skills

Some students with autism are unable to master an entire social interaction skill. The skill may therefore need to be task analyzed. Hence, to gear instruction effectively to individual students' needs, teachers and other instructors should define interaction skills along with their component parts. Once students have mastered the component parts, instruction on the entire skill may commence.

I. Consider the Importance of Setting and Material Variables

Introduction of skills into environments where they are most likely to occur and use of inherently interactive materials facilitates student learning and generalization. Accordingly, professionals should attempt to teach social skills in integrated classroom, home, and community settings, using play items and other materials that have natural interactive qualities. For instance, a group game might be taught effectively in a commons area, where students can functionally apply the skill with peers.

J. Consider Social Validity in Programming

Educators should question carefully whether or not an interaction skill will benefit a particular student with autism. Similarly, they should consider whether the skill will benefit others in the student's environment. That is, newly acquired skills should functionally enhance interactions between the student and others.

K. Prioritize Social Interaction Skills

Students with autism may require many instructional and practice sessions to incorporate a new skill into their repertoire. Professionals should first address social interaction skills having the greatest potential impact. In particular, they should attempt to select social interaction skills that can be used with a variety of people and settings.

L. Tailor Reinforcement to Meet Individual Needs

Teachers should tailor types and schedules of reinforcement to individual students' needs. Whenever possible, social reinforcers should be used. Thus, students who respond to social praise should not be introduced to tangible reinforcement. Educators should have plans and schedules for advancing students from one reinforcement type to another.

M. Educate Tutors and Others About Autism

Students with autism have characteristics and behaviors that teachers and regular class students may not be aware of. Thus, in order to facilitate interactions with autistic students, regular education staff and students should be provided opportunities to learn about autism. By promoting an understanding of autism and helping peers and teachers develop a positive attitude toward individuals with disabilities, social interaction programs are enhanced. Ideally, regular class students and teachers should know the characteristics of autism and have opportunities to become acquainted with autistic children and youth before formal social interaction programs are initiated.

N. Facilitate Initial Interactions

Teachers must make a concerted effort to ensure that prompts do not interfere with or disrupt social interactions. Students with autism often become prompt dependent; that is, they only respond or initiate after receiving a cue from their teacher. Hence, teachers should carefully monitor prompts to ensure that they facilitate rather than inhibit interactions and that they are applied as minimally as possible.

O. Make Data-Based Program Decisions

Professionals should collect and analyze data on the social interactions of regular class students with their peers with autism, both in structured and unstructured settings. Data analysis helps instructors to decide whether specific programs are effective and whether they require modification. Decisions relating to social interaction programs made independent of objective data are often faulty.

P. Generalize Social Skills

Students with autism may learn to use a social interaction skill in a specific setting or under a certain condition, but not understand that it has utility in other environments or circumstances. Therefore, it is important to plan for generalization of social interaction skills across individuals and settings. Without generalization instruction and practice, social interaction skills will typically be narrowly applied by children and youth with autism.

Q. Maintain Acquired Social Skills

Social interaction programs often are structured to teach a particular skill to mastery. Subsequent to criterion achievement, teachers move to another skill. However, if previously acquired skills are not reviewed, students may "forget" and eventually require new instruction. To limit such occurrences, teachers should provide opportunities for students with autism to practice and maintain previously acquired skills.

References

Bem, J. D., & Lord, C. G. (1979). Template matching: A proposal for probing the ecological validity of experimental settings in social psychology. *Journal of Personality and Social Psychology, 37,* 833–846.

Blew, P. A., Schwartz, I. S., & Luce, S. C. (1985). Teaching functional community skills to autistic children using nonhandicapped peer tutors. *Journal of Applied Behavior Analysis, 18,* 337–342.

Breen, C., Haring, T. G., Pitts-Conway, V., & Gaylord-Ross, R. (1985). The training and generalization of social interaction during breaktime at two job sites in the natural environment. *Journal of the Association for Persons for Severe Handicaps, 10,* 41–50.

Egel, A. L., Richman, G. S., & Koegel, R. L. (1981). Normal peer models and autistic children's learning. *Journal of Applied Behavior Analysis, 14,* 3–12.

Fiedler, C., & Simpson, R. (1987). Modifying the attitudes of nonhandicapped high school students toward handicapped peers. *Exceptional Children, 53,* 342–345.

Fox, J. J., Gunter, P., Brady, M. P., Bambara, L. M., Spiegel-McGill, P., & Shores, R. E. (1984). Using multiple peer exemplars to develop generalized social responding of an autistic girl. *Monograph in Behavioral Disorders, 7,* 17–26.

Fox, J. J., Shores, R. E., Linderman, D., & Strain, P. (1986). The effects of response dependent fading procedures in developing and maintaining social initiations of withdrawn preschool children. *Journal of Abnormal Child Psychology, 14,* 387–396.

Gaylord-Ross, R., & Haring, T. (1987). Social interaction research for adolescents with severe handicaps. *Behavioral Disorders, 12,* 264–275.

Gaylord-Ross, R. J., Haring, T. G., Breen, C., & Pitts-Conway, V. (1984). The training and generalization of social interaction skills with autistic youth. *Journal of Applied Behavior Analysis, 17,* 229–247.

Gaylord-Ross, R. J., & Pitts-Conway, V. (1984). Social behavior development in integrated secondary autistic programs. In N. Certo, N. Haring, & R. York (Eds.), *Public school integration of severely handicapped students* (pp. 197–221). Baltimore, MD: Brookes.

Gilliam, J. (1981). *Autism: Diagnosis, instruction, management and research.* Springfield, IL: Charles C Thomas.

Goldstein, H., & Strain, P. S. (1988). Peers as communication interventions agents: Some new strategies and research findings. *Topics in Language Disorders, 9*(1), 44–57.

Guess, D., & Siegel-Causey, E. (1985). Behavioral control and education of severely handicapped students: Who's doing what to whom? And why? In D. Bricker & J. Filler (Eds.), *Severe mental retardation: From theory to practice* (pp. 230–244). Reston, VA: The Council for Exceptional Children.

Kamps, D., Locke, P., Delquadri, J., & Hall, R. V. (1989). Increasing academic skills of students with autism using fifth grade peers as tutors. *Education and Treatment of Children, 12,* 38–51.

Kanner, L. (1943). Autistic disturbances of affective content. *Nervous Child, 2,* 217–250.

Kanner, L. (1971). Follow-up study of eleven autistic children originally reported in 1943. *Journal of Autism and Childhood Schizophrenia, 1*(2), 119–145.

Kazdin, A. E. (1977). Assessing the clinical or applied importance of behavior change through social validation. *Behavior Modification, 1,* 427–452.

Koegel, R., Rincover, A., & Egel, A. (1982). *Educating and understanding autistic children.* San Diego: College-Hill.

Kohler, F. W., & Greenwood, C. R. (1986). Toward a technology of generalization: The identification of natural contingencies of reinforcement. *The Behavior Analyst, 9,* 19–26.

Lord, C., & Hopkins, J. M. (1986). The social behavior of autistic children with younger and same-age nonhandicapped peers. *Journal of Autism and Developmental Disorders, 16*(3), 249–262.

Lovaas, O. I. (1987). Behavioral treatment and normal educational and intellectual functioning in young autistic children. *Journal of Consulting and Clinical Psychology, 55*(1), 3–9.

McConnell, S. R. (1987). Entrapment effects and the generalization and maintenance of social skills training for elementary school students with behavioral disorders. *Behavioral Disorders, 12,* 252–26.

McEvoy, M. A., & Odom, S. L. (1987). Social interaction training for preschool children with behavioral disorders. *Behavioral Disorders, 12*(4), 242–251.

Meyer, L. H., Fox, A., Schermer, A., Ketelsen, D., Montan, N., Maley, K., & Cole, D. (1987). The effects of teacher intrusion on social play interactions between children with autism and their nonhandicapped peers. *Journal of Autism and Developmental Disorders, 17*, 315–332.

Neel, R. (1986). Teaching functional social skills to children with autism. *Focus on Autistic Behavior, 1*(5), 1–8.

Odom, S. L., Hoyson, M., Jamieson, B., & Strain, P. S. (1985). Increasing handicapped preschoolers' peer social interactions: Cross-setting and component analysis. *Journal of Applied Behavior Analysis, 18*, 3–16.

Odom, S. L., & Strain, P. S. (1986). A comparison of peer-initiation and teacher-antecedent interventions for promoting reciprocal social interaction of autistic preschoolers. *Journal of Applied Behavior Analysis, 19*(1), 59–71.

Odom, S. L., Strain, P. S., Karger, M. A., & Smith, J. D. (1986). Using single and multiple peers to promote social interaction of preschool children with handicaps. *Journal of the Division for Early Childhood, 10*, 53–64.

Peck, C. A. (1985). Increasing opportunities for social control by children with autism and severe handicaps: Effects on student behavior and perceived classroom climate. *The Journal of the Association for Persons with Severe Handicaps, 10*(4), 183–193.

Ragland, E. U., Kerr, M. M., & Strain, P. S. (1978). Behavior of withdrawn autistic children. *Behavior Modification, 2*, 565–578.

Rumsey, J. M., Rapoport, J. L., & Sceery, W. R. (1985). Autistic children as adults: Psychiatric, social and behavioral outcomes. *Journal of the American Academy of Child Psychiatry, 24*, 465–473.

Rutter, M., & Schopler, E. (1987). Autism and pervasive developmental disorders: Concepts and diagnostic issues. *Journal of Autism and Developmental Disorders, 17*(2), 159–186.

Sasso, G. M. (1987). Social interactions: Issues and procedures. *Focus on Autistic Behavior, 2*(4), 1–7.

Sasso, G. M. (1989). *Promoting social relationships in individuals with autism.* Paper presented at the meeting of the Council for Children with Behavioral Disorders, Charlotte, NC.

Sasso, G. M., Hughes, G. F., Swanson, H. L., & Novak, C. G. (1987). A comparison of peer initiation interventions in promoting multiple peer initiators. *Education and Training in Mental Retardation, 22,* 150–155.

Sasso, G. M., Melloy, K. J., & Kavale, K. A. (1990). Generalization, maintenance, and behavioral covariation associated with social skill training through structured learning. *Behavioral Disorders, 16*(1), 9–22.

Sasso, G. M., Mitchell, V. N., & Struthers, E. M. (1986). Peer tutoring versus structured interaction activities: Effects on the frequency and topography of peer initiations. *Behavioral Disorders, 11,* 249–259.

Sasso, G. M., & Rude, H. A. (1987). Unprogrammed effects of training high-status peers to interact with severely handicapped children. *Journal of Applied Behavior Analysis, 20,* 35–44.

Sasso, G. M., Simpson, R., & Novak, C. (1985). Procedures for facilitating integration of autistic children in public school settings. *Analysis and Intervention in Developmental Disabilities, 5,* 233–246.

Schopler, E., & Mesibov, G. B. (Eds.). (1983). *Autism in adolescents and adults.* New York: Plenum.

Shapiro, T., Chiarandini, I., & Fish, B. (1974). Thirty severely disturbed children: Evaluation of their language development for classification and prognosis. *Archives of General Psychiatry, 30,* 819–825.

Shores, R. E. (1987). Overview of research on social interaction: A historical and personal perspective. *Behavioral Disorders, 12*(4), 233–241.

Simpson, R. L. (1987). Social interactions of behaviorally disordered children and youth: Where are we and where do we need to go? *Behavioral Disorders, 12,* 292–298.

Simpson, R., & Regan, M. (1986). *Management of autistic behavior.* Austin, TX: Pro-Ed.

Stokes, T., & Baer, D. (1977). An implicit technology of generalization. *Journal of Applied Behavior Analysis, 10,* 349–367.

Strain, P. S. (1982). Peer-mediated treatment of exceptional children's social withdrawal. In P. S. Strain (Ed.), *Social development of exceptional children* (pp. 93–105). Rockville, MD: Aspen.

Strain, P. S. (1983). Generalization of autistic children's social behavior change: Effects of developmentally integrated and segregated settings. *Analysis and Intervention in Developmental Disabilities, 3,* 23–34.

Strain, P. S., Cooke, T. P., & Apolloni, T. (1976). *Teaching exceptional children: Assessing and modifying social behavior.* New York: Academic Press.

Strain, P. S., & Fox, J. J. (1981). Peer social initiations and modification of social withdrawal: A review and future perspective. *Journal of Pediatric Psychology, 6*, 417–433.

Strain, P. S., Odom, S. L., & McConnell, S. (1984). Promoting social reciprocity of exceptional children: Identification, target behavior selection, and intervention. *Remedial and Special Education, 5*(1), 21–28.

Strain, P. S., Shores, R., & Kerr, M. M. (1976). An experimental analysis of spillover effects on the social interaction of behaviorally handicapped preschool children. *Journal of Applied Behavior Analysis, 9*, 31–40.

Strain, P. S., Shores, R. E., & Timm, M. A. (1977). Effects of peer social initiations on the behavior of withdrawn preschool children. *Journal of Applied Behavior Analysis, 10*, 289–298.

Strain, P. S., & Timm, M. A. (1974). An experimental analysis of social interactions between a behaviorally disordered preschool child and her classroom peers. *Journal of Applied Behavior Analysis, 7*, 583–590.

Tsai, L., & Scott-Miller, D. (1988). Higher-functioning autistic disorder. *Focus on Autistic Behavior,* 2(6), 1–8.

Twardosz, S., Nordquist, V. M., Simon, R., & Botkin, D. (1983). The effect of group affection activities on the interaction of socially isolate children. *Analysis and Intervention in Developmental Disabilities, 13*, 311–338.

Voeltz, C. M. (1982). Effects of structured interaction with severely handicapped peers on children's attitudes. *American Journal of Mental Deficiency, 86*, 180–190.

Wehman, P., & Kregel, J. (1988). Supported competitive employment for individuals with autism and severe retardation: Two case studies. *Focus on Autistic Behavior,* 3(3), 1–11.